Beethoven

Wise Publications
London/New York/Paris/Sydney/
Copenhagen/Madrid

£7·95

Exclusive Distributors:
Music Sales Limited
8/9 Frith Street, London W1V 5TZ, England.
Music Sales Pty Limited
120 Rothschild Avenue, Rosebery, NSW 2018, Australia.

This book © Copyright 1993 by
Wise Publications
Order No. AM91042
ISBN 0-7119-3366-9

Music processed by Interactive Sciences Limited, Gloucester
Book design by Hutton Staniford
Music arranged by Stephen Duro
Compiled by Peter Evans

Music Sales' complete catalogue lists thousands of titles and is free from your local music shop,
or direct from Music Sales Limited. Please send a cheque/postal order for £1.50 for postage to:
Music Sales Limited, Newmarket Road, Bury St. Edmunds, Suffolk IP33 3YB.

Your Guarantee of Quality
As publishers, we strive to produce every book to the highest commercial standards.

The music has been freshly engraved and the book has been carefully designed to minimise
awkward page turns and to make playing from it a real pleasure.

Particular care has been given to specifying acid-free, neutral-sized paper which has not been
chlorine bleached but produced with special regard for the environment. Throughout, the printing
and binding have been planned to ensure a sturdy, attractive publication which should give
years of enjoyment.

If your copy fails to meet our high standards, please inform us and we will gladly replace it.

Printed in the United Kingdom by
Halstan & Co Limited, Amersham, Buckinghamshire.

German Dance

5

Minuet In G

Song: Die Liebe Des Nächsten
(Brotherly Love)

Moderately

1st Movement Theme from Piano Sonata

Op. 26

Moderately

1st Movement Themes from Symphony No. 5

Fairly fast

16

2nd Movement Theme from Piano Sonata No. 2

Op. 14

2nd Movement Theme from Piano Sonata (Pathétique)
Op. 13

Moderately

2nd Movement Theme from Piano Sonata
Op. 90

Not too fast

3rd Movement Theme from Piano Concerto No. 1 in C (Rondo)

Op. 15

2nd Movement Theme from Symphony No. 7

28

4th Movement Theme from Symphony No. 6 (The Pastoral)

30

Last Movement Theme from Symphony No. 9 (Ode To Joy)

With movement

1st Movement Themes from Piano Concerto No. 3 in C Minor

Op. 37

Moderately fast

1st Movement Themes from Symphony No. 6 (The Pastoral)

Slow Movement Theme from Symphony No. 5

Theme from Moonlight
Sonata No. 2
Op. 27

Turkish March
From The Ruins Of Athens

4/99 (33949)